The Life
and Work
of...

Cézanne

Sean Connolly

Heinemann
LIBRARY

First published in Great Britain by
Heinemann Library,
Halley Court, Jordan Hill, Oxford OX2 8EJ
a division of Reed Educational and Professional
Publishing Ltd.
Heinemann is a registered trademark of Reed
Educational & Professional Publishing Ltd.

OXFORD   MELBOURNE   AUCKLAND
JOHANNESBURG   BLANTYRE   GABORONE
IBADAN   PORTSMOUTH (NH)   USA   CHICAGO

Designed by Celia Floyd
Illustrations by Karin Littlewood
Printed in Hong Kong/China

04 03 02 01 00
10 9 8 7 6 5 4 3 2 1

ISBN 0 431 09190 0
This title is also available in a hardback library
edition (ISBN 0 431 09182 X).

British Library Cataloguing in Publication Data

Connolly, Sean
    Life and work of Paul Cézanne
    1. Cézanne, Paul, 1839-1906 – Juvenile literature
    2. Painters – France – Biography – Juvenile literature
    3. Painting, Modern, 19th century – France – Juvenile
    literature
    4. Painting, French – Juvenile literature
    I. Title
    759.4

Acknowledgements

The Publishers would like to thank the following for
permission to reproduce photographs:

Page 4, Portrait photograph of Paul Cézanne, 1889,
Credit: AKG. Page 5, Paul Cézanne 'Self-Portrait
with beret', Credit: B & U International Picture
Service. Page 7, Paul Cézanne 'Sketchbook studies',
Credit: R.M.N/Michele Bellot. Page 9, Paul Cézanne
'Paul Alexis reading to Emile Zola', Credit:
Giraudon. Page 11, Paul Cézanne 'Portrait of
Pissarro', Credit: Giraudon. Page 12, Boulevard des
Capucines, Credit: Hulton Getty. Page 13, Paul
Cézanne 'Landscape, Auvers', Credit: Philadelphia
Museum of Art. Page 15, Paul Cézanne 'L'Etang des
Sœurs, Orsy', Credit: Courtauld Institute. Page 17,
Paul Cézanne 'The Blue Vase', Credit: Giraudon.
Page 19, Paul Cézanne 'The Pool at the Jas de
Bouffan', Credit: Metroplitan Museum of Art. Page
21, Paul Cézanne 'The Card Players', Credit: The
Bridgeman Art Library/Metropolitan Museum of
Art. Page 25, Paul Cézanne 'Portrait of Ambroise
Vollard', Credit: Giraudon. Page 26, Mont Sainte-
Victoire, Credit: Corbis. Page 27, Paul Cézanne
'Mont Sainte-Victoire', Credit: Philadelphia
Museum of Art. Page 28, Portrait photograph of
Cézanne in front of the picture 'Grand Bathers',
Credit: Giraudon. Page 29, Paul Cézanne 'En
Batau', Credit: National Museum of Western Art,
Tokyo.

Cover photograph reproduced with permission of
Index/Bridgeman Art Library.

Our thanks to Paul Flux for his comments in the
preparation of this book.

For more information about Heinemann Library
books, or to order, please telephone
+44(0)1865 888066, or send a fax to +441865 314091.
You can visit our web site at www.heinemann.co.uk

Any words appearing in the text in bold, **like this**,
are explained in the Glossary.

Contents

Who was Paul Cézanne?

Paul Cézanne was a painter who used colours and shapes to paint pictures of nature. He helped change the way artists look at things and paint them.

Cézanne painted this **portrait** of himself when he was about 60 years old. By that time he had had ideas about painting that would change the world of art.

Early years

Paul Cézanne was born on 19 January 1839 in Aix-en-Provence, France. One of his childhood friends was called Emile Zola. The boys loved to hike in the countryside near by.

Paul **studied** drawing when he was a teenager. He often drew pictures on his walks in the country. These drawings show how he was interested in nature.

Life in Paris

Paul wanted to be an artist but his father wanted him to be a lawyer. When Paul was 22 years old, his father gave him some money to move to Paris and be a painter.

Paul's friend Emile Zola had become a famous writer in Paris. He liked Paul's work and told other people about it. This painting shows a friend of Paul's reading to Emile.

Swapping ideas

In Paris, Paul became very friendly with a painter called Camille Pissarro. Together they would go to Camille's country house, to paint outside. These trips reminded Paul of home.

Paul did this **sketch** of Camille Pissarro in 1874. It shows how the painters would pack their things and hike to a favourite spot to paint.

Brush with fame

A group of painters called the **Impressionists** liked Paul's paintings. They showed two of his paintings at their first **exhibition** in 1874 in Paris. The exhibition was in a building in this street.

This **landscape** from the exhibition shows how
Paul used strong colours. The patches of light and
dark help to show the shape of the houses.

Ideas of his own

Paul began to try different ways of painting.
Patterns of colour and shape were more
important to Paul than exact copies of a **scene**.

Paul did this painting when he was aged 38. It uses thick, rough patches of paint to show how he saw a woodland pond.

Between two worlds

Paul also **studied** the work of the great artists of the past. He liked the French and Dutch artists who had lived more than 200 years before him.

The artists of the past had loved **still life** painting. Paul's painting of a blue vase shows that he loved it, too.

New freedom

Paul's father died in 1886 and Paul **inherited** enough money to live well. Now he did not have to worry about whether people would buy his paintings or not.

This meant that Paul was now free to do the paintings he wanted to do, in new ways. This **landscape** uses small blocks of colour to build a picture.

Ordinary people

Even though he was rich, Paul still thought of himself as ordinary. He painted other ordinary people and used his ideas about colour and shape.

This is one of many pictures Paul painted of card players. Although he was painting people, Paul saw the **scene** as a pattern of colours.

Southern sunshine

Paul began to spend more time near his childhood home. Here he **studied** the way that the sun changed the colour of the countryside.

Paul liked to paint a mountain called Mont Sainte-Victoire. This painting shows how he used colour to show distance as well as shapes.

Turning to people

Ambroise Vollard, an **art dealer** in Paris, had a successful **exhibition** of Paul's paintings in 1895. At the same time Paul began work on some **portraits**.

This is a portrait of Ambroise Vollard. Paul worked hard on each painting. He never finished this one, even though Ambroise had to **pose** for it 115 times!

A favourite view

Paul still worked mainly in the south of France. He still painted Mont Sainte-Victoire to show his ideas about colour, light and shape.

This view of the mountain in 1904 shows how Paul's work had changed. The mountain has become just a **blurred** pattern of colour.

Cézanne's last years

As he grew old, Paul still painted. He even ordered new paintbrushes just before he died in 1906, aged 67. By this time people knew he was a great painter.

In 1905 Paul did this painting of a group of people. It was done in **watercolour**. This type of painting was less tiring for Paul as he got older.

Timeline

1839   Paul Cézanne born in Aix-en-Provence, France on 19 January.

1840   The artist Claude Monet is born.

1845   The artist Mary Cassatt is born.

1853   The artist Vincent van Gogh is born.

1861   Paul moves to Paris to become a painter.

1861-5   Civil War in the United States.

1860s   Paul learns more about painting from his friend Camille Pissarro.

1870-1   War between France and Germany.

1871   Paul begins to paint outside to see light and colour more clearly.

1874   Paul has two paintings shown in the first **Impressionist Exhibition**.

1876   Alexander Graham Bell invents the telephone.

1879   The artist Paul Klee is born.

1886   Paul's father dies.

1890   The artist Vincent van Gogh dies.

1893   Lumière brothers develop cinema in France.

1895   Ambroise Vollard sets up a one-man exhibition of Cézanne paintings.

1898   The sculptor Henry Moore is born.

1902   Paul builds new **studio** to view Mont Saint-Victoire.

1903   Wright brothers fly the first aeroplane in the United States.

1906   Paul Cézanne dies in Aix-en-Provence on 22 October.

Glossary

art dealer   someone who sells paintings

blur   unclear or fuzzy

exhibition   public showing of paintings

Impressionists   group of artists who painted colourful outdoor pictures

inherit   receive money when someone dies

landscape   painting of the countryside

portrait   painting of a person

pose   to sit or stand still while being drawn

scene   place or area

sketch   another word for a drawing

still life   painting of things that are on a table

study   learn about a subject

watercolour   type of paint that is mixed with water and can be used quickly

More books to read

Changing Colour, Looking at pictures, Joy Richardson, Franklin Watts

Famous Lives: Artists, Jillian Powell, Wayland Publishers

More paintings to see

Zola's house, Paul Cézanne, Burrell Collection, Glasgow

Still Life with Water Jug, Paul Cézanne, Tate Gallery, London

The Gardener Vallier, Paul Cézanne, Tate Gallery, London

Index